SOLVING MYSTERIES WITH SCIENCE

CROP CIRCLES

JANE BINGHAM

Raintree

Chicago, Illinois

© 2013 Heinemann Raintree
an imprint of Capstone Global Library, LLC
Chicago, Illinois

To contact Capstone Global Library please
phone 800-747-4992, or visit our website
www.capstonepub.com

Edited by Adam Miller and Abby Colich
Designed by Marcus Bell
Original illustrations (pages 7, 11, 15) © Chris King
2013
All other original illustrations © Capstone Global
Library
Illustrated by Chris King and HL Studios
Picture research by Mica Brancic
Originated by Capstone Global Library, Ltd.
Printed in China by Leo Paper Group

16 15 14 13 12
10 9 8 7 6 5 4 3 2 1

**Library of Congress Cataloging-in-Publication
Data**
Bingham, Jane.
  Crop circles / Jane Bingham.
     p. cm.—(Solving mysteries with science)
  Includes bibliographical references and index.
  ISBN 978-1-4109-4988-2 (hbk.)—ISBN 978-1-4109-
4993-6 (pbk.) 1. Crop circles—Juvenile literature. 2.
Curiosities and wonders—Juvenile literature. I. Title.
  AG243.B488 2013
  001.94—dc23   2012012697

Acknowledgments

The author and publisher are grateful to the following
for permission to reproduce copyright material:
Alamy: p. 43 main (© David Newham); AP/Press
Association Images: p. 42 (Keystone/Sandro
Campardo); Corbis: pp. 20 (All Canada Photos/©
David Nunuk), 23 (Science Faction/© Tony Hallas),
24 (JAI/© Nigel Pavitt), 26 (epa/© Vladislav
Galgonek), 27 (© Mike Agliolo), 28 (© Sandro
Vannini); Getty Images: pp. 34 (Taxi/Birgid Allig), 37
(Photolibrary/Jacob Halaska); Rex Features: pp. 5 (M
& Y Agency Ltd), 18 (Christopher Jones), 30 (Mike
Walker), 36 (Steve Alexander), 39 (Mike Walker), 40,
41 (Steve Alexander); Science Photo Library: pp. 35
(David Parker), 38 (David Parker); Shutterstock: pp.
21 (© Péter Gudella), 22 (© Jezper), 26 top right (©
colia), 29 (© Natalia Mylova), 29 (© Ra Studio), 31
inset (© Antonio S.), 31 main (© Norph), 32 (© Iakov
Kalinin), 33 (© olly), 43 inset top (© Eric Isselée).

Cover photograph mathematic formula in crop circle
reproduced with permission from Rex Features (Mike
Walker).

Design feature images: Shutterstock

Every effort has been made to contact copyright
holders of any material reproduced in this book. Any
omissions will be rectified in subsequent printings if
notice is given to the publisher.

Contents

What Are Crop Circles?

For centuries, people have been amazed and puzzled by crop circles. All over the world, circles and other patterns have suddenly appeared in fields of crops. Some crop circles are simple, circular shapes. Others are incredibly elaborate. These complex crop formations can take the form of patterns, diagrams, or pictures drawn on the ground. But whatever shape they take, nobody has completely explained how or why they are formed.

Where and when?

Crop formations have appeared in the United States, Canada, Australia, Japan, India, and other parts of the world, but they are most often found in southern England. The earliest report of a crop circle dates from the 1600s, and there have been reports ever since. However, sightings of circles increased dramatically in the 1970s, especially in southern England. This made some people suspect that the circles were the work of hoaxers (people who created the circles as a joke).

Eyewitness accounts?

Most crop circles are discovered fully formed, leaving people to wonder how they could have been made. But in a few remarkable cases, there is an eyewitness. These witnesses describe the chilling experience of watching a pattern form in front of their eyes. Other people have questioned whether these accounts can be trusted, but the witnesses have stuck to their stories.

Can the mystery be solved?

In the first part of this book, you can read about people's strange experiences with crop circles. The second part takes a careful look at the theories behind the mystery and asks some questions. Do the theories really make sense? Have the so-called experts approached the problem in a scientific way? And can science solve the mystery of crop circles?

Solving the mystery

How are crop circles formed, and what do their patterns mean? People have come up with many explanations, but the mystery has never really been solved.

Crop formations

Crop circles are often known as crop formations. Crop formations can take the form of a simple disc or spiral, or they can be a complex design or even a picture. Crop formations showing designs or pictures are sometimes called pictograms.

SPIRALS AT STONEHENGE

On a sunny July afternoon in 1996, a pilot was flying his small passenger plane over southern England. His route took him directly over the prehistoric stone circle of Stonehenge. As he looked down on the circle of stones, he felt a shiver of awe and fear at this ancient mystery. Then he forgot all about it until his return flight.

SPIRALS IN A FIELD

Looking down again at the fields around Stonehenge, the pilot couldn't believe his eyes. Where there had been an empty field just an hour before, there was now a gigantic, swirling pattern. What on Earth was happening? And was there some connection between the prehistoric circle and the strange new pattern in the field?

AN EYEWITNESS ACCOUNT

For many years, nothing was known about how the circle was formed. Then, in 2009, an eyewitness told her story. She never gave her name, so she is simply known as Mrs. M. On the afternoon of July 7, 1996, she was driving past Stonehenge when she noticed a small group gathering in a field. Parking her car quickly, she ran to join the group, and was astonished by what she saw.

A CIRCLE OF MIST

A circle of mist was hovering over the ground at about waist height. It was spinning rapidly, flattening wheat stalks as it spun. Then the misty shape increased in size, creating larger and larger patterns in the field.

"THE STRANGEST THING I HAVE EVER SEEN"

Mrs. M. completely lost track of time. She believes she stood and stared for about 20 minutes before she finally staggered back to her car, leaving the circle of mist still hovering in the field. Later she said: "It was the strangest thing I have ever seen... I thought, 'Are we going to see a leprechaun or the men from Mars...?'"

WEIRD SENSATIONS

Soon people were flocking to see the new crop formation, and on July 9, Lucy Pringle arrived at the site.

She was an expert on crop circles and very eager to see the patterns—but some invisible force seemed to be holding her back.

It felt as if a warning voice was telling her, "Stay away!" So she returned to wait anxiously in her car.

It wasn't long before Lucy's friends came stumbling back to the car. She was shocked to see that they looked exhausted and had turned "pea green with nausea." But then, in front of her eyes, they started to recover, and very soon they were back to their normal selves again.

POWERFUL ENERGY?

Lucy's friends were not the only ones to feel the mysterious power of the circle. Two days later, a scientist named Callum felt his body being filled with some kind of powerful energy, which left him shaken and exhausted. Then these feelings were replaced by an even more alarming sensation. Callum realized that he was thinking much more clearly than he ever had before, as if some superpower had taken over his brain!

READING THE PATTERNS

The Stonehenge spirals certainly had some very unusual powers. But what did they mean? People were soon swapping theories excitedly. Mathematicians looked at the pattern and saw a "Julia set"—the diagram of a complex mathematical idea. Musicians saw a bass clef—a symbol used when writing down music. Some scientists saw the spiral shape found in shells and other natural forms. The patterns seemed to be some kind of puzzle set by a superhuman intelligence. But who or what could have created them?

FLYING SAUCERS?

Very few people have witnessed a crop circle being formed. One of the most dramatic accounts comes from Australia in 1966, when a farmer saw a sight that he would never forget...

THE SAUCER FROM THE SWAMP

It was a calm summer morning when George Pedley drove his tractor toward the shore of Horseshoe Lagoon, on a farm near Tully, in Queensland, Australia. George was a steady, hardworking young man, who was not the type to daydream at work. He was busy thinking of the tasks ahead when his thoughts were interrupted by a loud hissing sound. George brought his tractor to a sudden halt.

Then he gasped in disbelief. Could he really be seeing this?

Less than 25 yards (20 meters) away, something was rising slowly out of the swamp. It was large, gray, and misty—and it was shaped like a saucer!

THE SAUCER TAKES OFF

George gazed in amazement as the saucer hovered around tree level. Then, in front of his eyes, spinning fast, it rose to about 30 feet (10 meters) in the air.

Now George was desperate to see more, but before he could make a move, the saucer moved away again. Suddenly, it made a shallow swoop, before taking off at a tremendous speed. It then climbed steeply through the sky and gradually disappeared from view. Three hours later, George returned to the scene.

He found a massive circular mat in the exact place where the spacecraft had been hovering.

The mat was made of tightly woven water reeds, all bent in a clockwise direction. Who or what could have formed such a thing? George shivered to himself. It was time to share his discovery.

FLYING SAUCER NESTS?

Within a couple of days, the farm was swarming with investigators—and five more circular nests had been found. Some of the nests showed signs of burning at the center, and it was agreed that animals could not be responsible for making any of them. Soon all the newspapers were full of the news: "Flying saucer nests found at Tully!"

A BLAZING BALL

Did flying saucers make the Tully circles? We may never know. But there is another story that could support the idea of visitors from space...

On July 29, 1990, Steve Alexander was filming on Milk Hill, in southern England. Two crop circles had recently appeared in this area, so he was hoping to catch something on film. But what he managed to film was a complete surprise.

As Steve panned his camera over the fields, he spotted a blazing ball of light dropping down from the sky. He tracked the gleaming ball as it moved through the fields. Then, suddenly, the ball took off and flew toward a tractor, before disappearing into the distance. Many people are still mystified when watching what Steve filmed that day.

A SECOND WITNESS

Steve was not the only one to see the ball of light. Several months later, the tractor driver also described what he saw. He remembered a light in the sky "as big as a beach ball and glinting and flashing."

Was the glinting ball evidence of visitors from outer space? And could the visitors be responsible for the crop circles in the area?

THE FACE
IN THE FIELD

There was something spooky about the atmosphere around Crabwood Farm on the night of August 14, 2002. Usually the farm was a peaceful place, set in the gentle countryside of southern England. But on that warm summer night, weird things were happening...

OMINOUS SIGNS

One woman heard loud throbbing noises that sounded like a noisy engine. Another person noticed a strong, burning smell. Some local campers were amazed to see dancing lights in the sky. All of them felt uneasy about their experiences.

What could be happening out in the fields?

A SURPRISING SIGHT

The next day, a local woman was enjoying her usual morning horse ride past Crabwood Farm. Looking over the hedges, she saw a surprising sight. The farmer's wheat had been flattened into some enormous shapes! She was too close to see what the shapes could be, but she knew that something very peculiar had taken place.

FIGURING OUT THE PATTERN

By the following day, investigator Lucy Pringle was on the case. She had rented a plane to fly over Crabwood Farm, and soon she was busy taking photos. But as she looked down at the fields, Lucy was puzzled. The shapes laid out on the ground were completely different from the usual geometric patterns. What could they possibly show?

Lucy's confusion lasted until she reached home. Then, as she studied her photos, it suddenly dawned on her. She was staring into the face of an alien!

BREAKING THE CODE

Once Lucy recognized the alien face, it did not take long for her to realize that the disc beside it must hold some kind of message. But what could the symbols mean? It was time to contact the experts—a group of investigators, computer experts, and code-breakers who all set to work to solve the puzzle.

A MYSTERIOUS MESSAGE

Soon the team was hard at work, translating the symbols into digits, and feeding the digits into a computer. It was challenging work, but at last they came up with a mysterious message: "Beware the bearers of false gifts and their broken promises. Much pain but still time. There is good out there. We oppose deception. Conduit closing."

WHAT DID IT REALLY MEAN?

It was all very interesting, but what did it mean? Was it a message from aliens? And were the aliens trying to rescue humankind from a terrible fate? Or was it simply the work of some very clever hoaxers, who had created the pattern as some kind of joke? The mystery of the face in the field has not yet been solved.

Messages from space?

The crop formation at Crabwood Farm is similar to a pictogram found in 2001 at Chilbolton in Hampshire, England, less than 10 miles (16 kilometers) away. This formation showed a cat-like alien face and a set of symbols in a rectangular frame.

When the Chilbolton message was decoded, it seemed to be an answer to a radio message that had been sent into space from a giant radio telescope in Arecibo, Puerto Rico. The Aricebo message was intended to find out whether intelligent life existed in space. As the investigators realized what they were reading, they felt a thrill of excitement. Did the Chilbolton message prove that there really were aliens out in space?

Investigating Crop Circles

Can the mystery of crop circles be solved? People have put forward a range of different theories about how the circles are formed and what their patterns mean. But do these theories make sense? The next six chapters will examine these theories and put them to the test of science and common sense.

Studying the circles

Reports of crop circles date from the 1600s, but interest really took off in the 1970s, when individuals and teams began to conduct some serious scientific investigations. Some people simply described their theories, but many followed the scientific method (see box on page 19). Interest in crop circles reached its peak in the 1990s, and some investigators are still at work today.

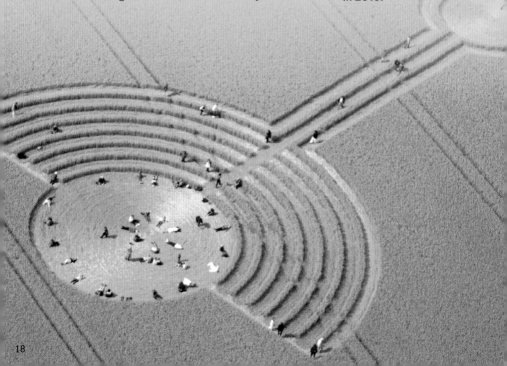

▼ People flock to this new crop formation in Wiltshire, England, in 2010.

The scientific method

Good investigators follow the scientific method when they need to establish and test a theory. The scientific method has five basic steps:

1. Make observations (comments based on studying something closely).
2. Do some background research.
3. Form a testable hypothesis. This is basically a prediction or "educated guess" to explain the observations.
4. Conduct experiments or find evidence to support the hypothesis.
5. After thinking carefully about the evidence, draw conclusions.

Ask question

Do background research

Think! Try again

Construct hypothesis

Test with an experiment

Analyze results. Draw conclusion

Hypothesis is true

Hypothesis is false or partially true

Report results

Cereologists, croppies, and circle chasers

People who investigate crop formations are known as cereologists. Their ideas and experiments are published in books and magazines and on the Internet. Followers of their theories have been nicknamed croppies or circle chasers. They follow the latest ideas and share their responses on blogs and social networking sites.

All sorts of crops

Crop circles are usually found in wheat fields. But they have also appeared in other crops, including oats, barley, rye, maize (corn), and rapeseed. They have even been found in rice fields and reed beds.

Mist and Lights

As you have read, some people claim that they have witnessed crop circles being made. These witnesses often describe swirling mists or strange lights in the sky. Most croppies believe that the mists and lights are caused by nonhuman energies. But are there other explanations for these changes in the atmosphere?

▲ An isolated patch of mist or fog can suddenly appear in a field and hover over the ground.

Mysterious mists

Some witnesses of crop circles have described a swirling mist that hovers over a field, causing the crops to bend and flatten. This is what Mrs. M reported in a field near Stonehenge in 1996 (see page 6). Can this phenomenon (strange happening) be explained by science?

Not so mysterious?

Mists are very common in the late summer months, when most crop circles appear, and they often form patches over fields (see the box). These patches of mist contain large amounts of water, making them heavy and moist. It is possible that a patch of mist could place some pressure on the crops. At the same time, some moisture could enter the crops, causing them to bend a little. However, there is no evidence that a mist could completely flatten an area of crops— and, even if it could, a mist could not form detailed patterns in a field.

How are mist patches formed?

Mist is formed when cold air passes over moist land. The cold air causes the moisture rising up from the earth to cool rapidly and condense (turn from a gas into a liquid), forming droplets of water. These water droplets hang in the air, creating patches of mist just above the ground.

Balls of light

Several people have claimed that they saw balls of light in the sky around the time that a crop circle was formed. There are even videos showing mysterious lights descending from the sky and moving over fields. One of the best-known film records was made by Steve Alexander near Milk Hill, in southern England (see page 13). Croppies suggest that these balls of light could be some kind of spacecraft, or even a mysterious energy mass from outer space. But can the lights in the sky be explained in other ways?

▼ Can crop circles really be linked to mysterious lights in the sky?

Myth-buster

Can you trust the evidence?

The Milk Hill video shows a small blob of light that travels just above the ground. Some croppies have claimed that this light could be some kind of alien spacecraft. However, this claim cannot be proven. A more common-sense approach to the video would suggest the blob resembles a light, shiny object (such as a balloon or a plastic bag) that is being blown by the wind. You can watch the video online and decide what you think.

Unreliable witnesses

Eyewitness reports cannot always be trusted. Witnesses may be overcome by powerful emotions, which prevent them from seeing things clearly. It is a good scientific practice to collect as many accounts (stories) as possible and compare them. If there is only one account, it should be treated with caution.

Other explanations

Moving lights in the sky at night could be meteors (commonly known as shooting stars). Meteoroids are lumps of rock from space that fall toward Earth and burn up as they enter Earth's atmosphere. Other explanations for moving lights include airplane lights and reflected spots of light from shiny surfaces.

Whirling Winds

Some accounts of crop circles include a description of a whirling wind that leaves a perfect pattern behind it. Croppies believe that these mysterious spinning columns of air contain some form of alien energy. But could there be a natural explanation instead?

Whirlwinds of all sizes

It is possible that some simple crop circles have been formed by whirlwinds. Whirlwinds are rotating columns of air that travel across the ground. They can range in size from towering tornadoes to dust eddies measuring about 3 feet (1 meter) high.

Whirlwinds occur in many parts of the world, but they are most common in areas of open ground. Small dust eddies often race across the large, open fields of southern and eastern England. These are areas where many crop circles are found.

▲ It is possible that a whirling eddy of dust could flatten a circular patch of crops. But is it likely that it could create a detailed pattern?

Whirlwind damage

Inside a whirlwind, pressure builds up very fast, and air is forced downward. Whirlwinds can cause serious damage, often flattening fences and tearing up plants. From this evidence, people have come to the conclusion that a small whirlwind could flatten a patch of crops.

This diagram shows how air is pushed downward in a circular pattern, as a whirlwind, or eddy, moves across the surface of the ground.

Watching the whirlwind

In 1990, Kathleen Skin described an experience that took place in Cambridgeshire, England, in 1934, when she was 14 years old. While she was standing in a field of corn, she saw "a whirlwind in the center of the field, spinning stalks, seeds, and dust up into the air for about 100 or more feet." Afterward, she found "a perfect circle of flattened corn, the stalks interlaced [woven together] and their ears lying on each other." She suggested that the circle was formed by "a sort of miniature tornado."

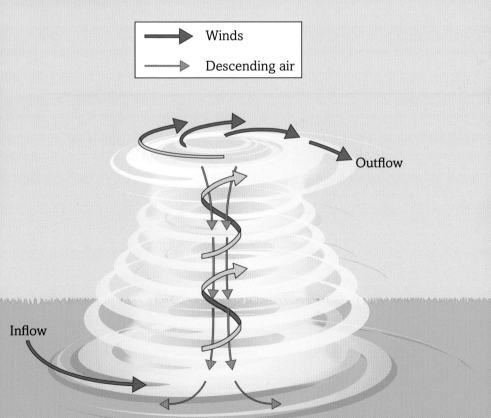

Winds

Descending air

Outflow

Inflow

Electricity inside the vortex

Whirlwinds create a vortex—a rapidly spinning flow of air. This vortex contains many tiny particles of dust. In the 1970s, Dr. Terence Meaden, an expert on storms, noted that particles in a vortex become charged with electricity as they are caught up in the spinning air. He named the particles *plasma*, the term used by scientists to mean electrically charged particles.

The plasma vortex theory

Meaden built on his understanding of a vortex to develop a theory for the creation of crop circles. According to Meaden's plasma vortex theory, the electrical particles in a vortex send powerful signals to the crops beneath them. These electrical signals are sent in a certain pattern. The pattern is reproduced in the crops, creating a swirling, spiral effect.

▼ Could this circle have been caused by electrical signals in a small whirlwind? These investigators are trying to find out.

▲ Does the plasma vortex theory provide a scientific explanation for reported sightings of UFOs?

Meaden also claimed that the particles inside a vortex can appear to glow as they become charged with electricity. He said this could explain the glowing lights that some people have seen near crop circles.

Does the theory stand up?

The plasma vortex theory appeared to provide a good explanation for the formation of simple crop circles. However, in the 1990s, many complex crop formations began to appear. Meaden did not believe that his theory could explain these complex formations. He came to the conclusion that these formations were hoaxes, and he abandoned his work on crop circles.

Testing the theory

The plasma vortex theory was tested following the scientific method. Two Japanese scientists, Dr. Y. H. Ohtsuki and Professor H. Ofuruton, created a model in their laboratory and conducted a series of experiments. Their results proved that Meaden's theory could provide a possible solution to the mystery of simple crop circles.

Mysterious Microwaves?

When people examined the plants inside crop circles, they found that their stalks had been gently bent, but not broken or snapped. This discovery made some cereologists curious. They were certain that if a hoaxer had flattened the crops, the stalks would have shown much more damage.

In the 1990s, Dr. William Levengood, a specialist in biophysics, decided to investigate what was happening to the plants. He launched an in-depth investigation called Project Argus.

▼ Not all scientists agree that the "softening" of crops inside crop circles is caused by energy waves (see page 31).

▲ Are the crops in crop circles softened like vegetables in a microwave oven?

How microwave energy works

Microwave ovens transmit microwaves. These are a type of electromagnetic wave similar to X-rays and radio waves (see page 45). The microwaves are absorbed by the water, fats, and sugars in food and are turned into heat. This means that food is warmed and softened on the inside, but not burned on the outside.

Microwaved crops?

Levengood began by examining the structure of plants in crop circles very carefully. He noted that the tissues (inside structures) of the wheat stalks seemed to have softened. He claimed that the tissues had changed in exactly the same way as tissues in vegetables soften in a microwave oven. Then he asked the question: What kind of energy could have caused this softening?

Gravitational vortex theory

Levengood returned to the plasma vortex theory (see page 26). He built on this idea to develop his own hypothesis, which he called his gravitational vortex theory. In Levengood's theory, the energy inside a wind vortex is similar to the energy waves produced by a microwave oven. Levengood claimed that these energy waves could gently heat and soften crops, in the same way that microwaves cook vegetables.

Energy from space?

In his gravitational vortex theory, Levengood states that crop circles are formed by a vortex of energy. But he does not believe that weather conditions on Earth are the cause of vortexes (or whirlwinds). Instead, he suggests that vortexes are created in the ionosphere.

The ionosphere is one of the layers in space, beyond Earth's atmosphere (see page 45). It is a region of powerful electrical energy. Levengood claims that the particles in a vortex are charged with electricity in the ionosphere before moving toward Earth.

Testing the theory

Over the course of 14 years, Levengood has examined more than 250 samples of plants. The plants were taken from crop circles and sent to his laboratory in Michigan. Then he examined them under a microscope and tested them to see if they had been affected by electromagnetic waves.

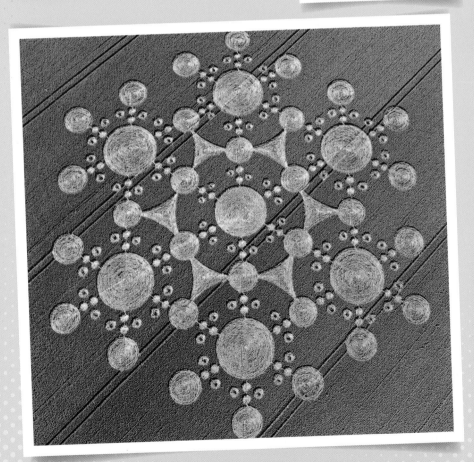

▲ Dr. Levengood claimed that small variations in electromagnetic energy can have different effects on crops. He said this explained complex pictograms.

In 2005, a group of scientists wrote an article that criticized Levengood for failing to follow the scientific method. The scientists claimed that Levengood did not collect his samples properly, and that he ignored results that did not fit his hypothesis. The scientists said the stalks that Levengood claimed had been affected by electromagnetic energy could simply have been flattened by a wooden board.

Myth-buster

Space dust or Earth dust?

Levengood found a type of dust inside crop circles that is also found in meteorites (the remains of rocks that fall from space). The dust is hematite, a form of iron. According to Levengood, this "space dust" provides scientific evidence for his theory that his vortexes were originally formed in the ionosphere. However, Levengood's "space dust" is not just found in space. Hematite is also very common on Earth.

▲ Are crop circles really caused by whirling particles of "space dust"?

Unusual Effects

Visitors to crop circles have reported some strange experiences. Some people have noticed that their cell phones have suddenly failed to operate. Others have described unusual physical symptoms. This chapter will look at the evidence for weird happenings inside crop circles.

▼ Some people claim that crop circles make them feel very strange. Can science explain their strange sensations?

Electrical interference?

In the early 1990s, there were several reports of problems with phones and video cameras inside crop circles. Some people claimed that mysterious energy waves were interfering with (interrupting) their electrical equipment. Cereologist Paul Vigay decided to conduct his own scientific investigation.

Vigay constructed electronic equipment that could pick up on very small flows of electrical current. Then he used his equipment to test stalks of wheat inside and outside a crop circle. Vigay discovered that the stalks outside the circle had a small electrical charge, while the stalks inside the circle had no charge at all. He came to the conclusion that the stalks in the circle had been affected by some kind of force that had drained away their electrical energy.

Can science explain it?

Is there a scientific explanation for Vigay's findings? Some people have linked Vigay's discovery with the ideas of Terence Meaden and William Levengood (see pages 26 to 31). Both these scientists proposed that crop formations are formed by some kind of electrical energy. If their hypothesis is correct, then it may be possible that this energy had an effect inside the circle.

Myth-buster

Unreliable signals

Many crop formations are found in remote (far-off), hilly areas where phone reception is patchy and it is hard to get a reliable signal. Perhaps this is the reason why people experience problems using their cell phones close to crop circles?

▶ Can mysterious energy waves really be to blame for bad phone reception?

All sorts of feelings

Many people say that they have experienced powerful feelings inside crop circles. Some have felt happy and peaceful or unusually clearheaded. Others have suffered from feelings of sickness, giddiness, and headaches, and some have become panicky or sad. Croppies claim that all these sensations are reactions to a powerful energy source. But can the reports be trusted?

Unreliable evidence?

Most people who visit crop formations have some belief in the paranormal. Even before they enter a circle, they are probably expecting to feel "different." This means that their reports cannot be completely reliable. It is also puzzling that some people have very positive sensations, while others feel only negative effects.

Hearing things

Some visitors to crop circles have reported hearing odd, high-pitched sounds. Some have described a high humming note. Others have heard a trilling noise. Some faint trilling sounds were recorded by cereologist Colin Andrews in 1989, during Operation White Crow, an investigation of a crop formation in Hampshire, England.

Can the sounds be explained?

Is there an explanation for the high-pitched noises? Some croppies have claimed that the sounds may be "harmonics"—music created by the energy source that formed the crop circles. More down-to-earth explanations are that the sounds are distant traffic, planes, machinery, or noises made by birds, insects, or animals.

Testing reactions

It would be possible to conduct an experiment on different reactions to crop circles. People could be asked before they entered a circle whether they believed in the paranormal or not. Then they could be questioned about the feelings they experienced in the circle. What would you predict the results would show?

▲ George Wingfield, shown here, is one of the leading investigators of crop formations.

Messages and Meanings?

Many croppies claim that crop formations contain important messages for human beings. They believe these messages are created by nonhuman forms of intelligence, and they devote lots of time and effort to figuring out what the messages might mean. Skeptics (nonbelievers) say that this is wasted effort, because hoaxers make the designs. This chapter will examine the arguments on both sides.

▼ This crop formation from 2011 uses a strange symbol.

▲ Mysterious symbols have been drawn on the ground for centuries. This design is one of many large-scale patterns, known as the Nazca lines, found in the deserts of Peru. The Nazca lines are about 2,000 years old. Some claim they were made by aliens.

Past messages?

Many crop formations include symbols drawn from ancient civilizations. Symbols used by the Aztecs, the Maya, the ancient Egyptians, and the Celts have all appeared in crop circles. Some croppies have suggested that the crop formations could be coded messages from the spirits of ancient peoples. Some of them believe that these ancient spirits are trying to make contact with people living in the present.

Jumbled symbols

Skeptics say that the symbols in crop formations cannot be pieced together to make a readable message. They claim that the symbols have been chosen by hoaxers simply because they look mysterious. They also point out that some crop formations combine symbols from a range of different civilizations. They say it is unlikely that all the ancient spirits are living and working together!

Powerful places?

Many crop formations are found near ancient sacred (holy) sites, such as prehistoric stone circles or burial chambers. Crop circles are also often found on ley lines (imaginary lines running through the landscape that are believed to connect places of spiritual power). But does the positioning of crop circles in places of spiritual power have any special meaning? Does it really suggest that the circles contain messages from ancient spirits? Or do hoaxers make a deliberate choice to create their circles in "spiritual" places?

Warnings from Earth?

Some croppies believe that crop formations may be messages from Gaia (see the box). They suggest that Gaia is warning humans that their time on Earth is running out.

Skeptics say that only a few crop formations can be interpreted as messages from Gaia. They also ask why Gaia would choose to send most of her messages to people in England, rather than to people across the globe!

A message from aliens?

In 2002, a crop formation appeared at Crabwood Farm, in Hampshire, England, that appeared to contain a coded message from an alien race (see pages 16 and 17). Croppies believed the message was an attempt by aliens to make contact with human begins. Skeptics saw it as the work of hoaxers.

Gaia: The spirit of Earth

The "Gaia hypothesis" was developed by British scientist James Lovelock. He claimed that all living things on planet Earth are linked together in a single organism (living thing), which he named Gaia. Lovelock said that Gaia was sick because of the damage that humans have done to Earth, and he explained that Gaia was trying to send warnings to humans.

▲ This formation shows a mathematical pattern known as the Mandelbrot set. It appeared in a field close to Cambridge University, in England, in 1991, at a time when researchers in Cambridge were exploring Mandelbrot's ideas. Skeptics claim that the crop formation was the work of the researchers or their friends.

A higher intelligence at work?

Some crop formations show very complex mathematical ideas. Croppies claim that these detailed designs must be the work of a higher, nonhuman intelligence. But skeptics ask some common-sense questions. Why should nonhumans be working on the same mathematical problems as humans? And why would they choose to do their calculations in the middle of a field, millions of miles away from home?

▲ This dramatic crop formation shows a mathematical idea, known as the Euler Theorem. It appeared in a field of yellow rapseed at Wilton in Wiltshire, England, in May 2010.

Hoaxers and Circle-Makers

Some crop circles are known to be the work of hoaxers. Hoaxers create crop formations as a kind of game, working secretly and leaving no clues behind them. A few hoaxers have revealed themselves. But most have never told their secrets. This means that people have to guess whether a crop formation is a hoax or not.

Doug and Dave

The most famous hoaxers are Doug Bower and Dave Chorley. In 1991, they claimed that they had made over 200 crop circles in southern England between 1978 and 1991. Bower and Chorley explained that they made their designs using a plank of wood attached to a piece of string. But not everyone was convinced. It has been estimated that it would take several days to stake out a complex design in a field and then create it. So it seems very unlikely that just two men could have designed and made over 200 formations.

▲ In 1991, Doug Bower and Dave Chorley admitted that they were hoaxers. Here they demonstrate how they planned one of their crop formations.

Art and promotion

Not all crop circles are made in secret. Since the 1990s, teams of circle-makers have been producing crop formations as works of art or as dramatic stunts. TV and radio stations and food companies have paid for super-sized advertisements to be created in fields.

All in one place

Crop circles are very common in southern England, and most of these are found in the counties of Hampshire and Wiltshire. This evidence suggests that the circles must be the work of one or more teams of hoaxers based in southern England.

However, cereologists have produced another argument. They say that southern England has many prehistoric sites, making it very rich in the spiritual energy that is needed to form crop circles.

▼ Many crop circles appear close to ancient stone circles, which some people believe are a source of spiritual power.

Can the Mystery Be Solved?

Is it possible to explain how crop circles are formed? Are they all the work of hoaxers? Or could some of the circles have other causes?

Simple explanations

People have come up with several explanations for simple crop circles. They suggest that these simple discs or spirals may have been created by whirlwinds. They also claim that mists and thunderstorms could explain the unusual sights and sounds that have been reported near crop formations. In a few cases, it has been suggested that animals, such as hedgehogs, could have flattened the crops to form a circle.

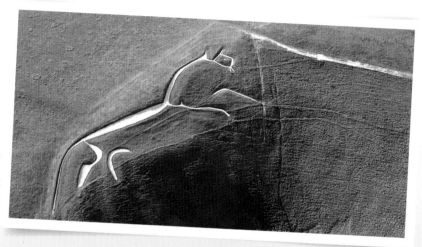

▲ There are many unsolved mysteries in our landscape. This ancient design, known as the Uffington white horse, was obviously the work of humans, but no one knows exactly what its purpose was. Scientists think it is about 3,000 years old.

Exciting solutions

Cereologists have proposed some exciting solutions to the mystery. Dr. Terence Meaden claimed that simple crop circles may have been created by a whirling vortex filled with electrically charged particles. Dr. William Levengood took these ideas one step further. He claimed that the whirling vortexes were originally formed outside Earth's atmosphere, and that they traveled down to Earth from space.

Many cereologists believe that crop circles are formed by powerful sources of spiritual energy. They suggest that this energy could be linked to past civilizations or to Gaia, the spirit of Earth. Some croppies have even suggested that crop formations contain coded messages from alien races.

What do you think?

Do you think that all crop formations are caused by hoaxers? Or do you believe that there is still a mystery to be explained? Perhaps you think that some of the theories in this book provide the right answers? In the end, it is up to you to make up your own mind about crop circles.

Timeline

BCE

c. 2700
The Stonehenge stone circle is constructed in Wiltshire, England.

c. 1400–600
The white horse design is created at Uffington, Berkshire, in England.

CE

200 BCE–600 CE
Nazca lines are created in the Nazca deserts in southern Peru.

1686
Robert Plot records circles and patterns found in fields in *A Natural History of Staffordshire*.

1880
J. Rand Capron writes to the journal *Nature* to describe crop circles found in southern England.

1966
A report of a "flying saucer" is followed by the discovery of "saucer nests" near Tully, in Australia.

1974
A report of a "flying saucer" is followed by the discovery of circles near Langenburg, in Saskatchewan, Canada.

1980s
Dr. Terence Meaden develops his plasma vortex theory to explain how crop circles are made.

1989
Colin Andrews leads Operation White Crow to investigate a crop circle in Hampshire, England.

1990s
Dr. William Levengood develops his gravitational vortex theory to explain how crop circles are made. Paul Vigay tests crop circles for the presence of electrical currents.

1990
Steve Alexander films a ball of light near Milk Hill, Wiltshire, in England.

1991
A crop formation showing the mathematical "Mandlebrot set" appears near Cambridge, England.

1991
Doug Bower and Dave Chorley claim to have made over 200 crop circles in southern England.

1994
A crop formation known as the "galaxy" appears at Alton Barnes, in England.

1996
A crop formation showing the mathematical "Julia set" appears near Stonehenge, in England.

2001
An alien face and message panel appear at Chilbolton, Hampshire, in England.

2002
An alien face and message disc appear at Crabwood Farm, in England.

2003
A crop formation showing the first 10 digits of pi is found in Wiltshire, England.

2010
A crop formation showing the Euler mathematical theorem appears in Wiltshire, England.

Summing Up the Science

Two main theories have been suggested to explain how crop circles are made. One is the plasma vortex theory (see pages 26 and 27). The other is the gravitational vortex theory (see pages 28 to 31). Most scientists do not agree with these theories. Nevertheless, it is worth taking a careful look at some of the scientific ideas that lie behind them.

Electro-magnetic waves

Both the vortex theories claim that crop circles are created by some form of electromagnetic energy. But what exactly does this mean?

Electromagnetic waves are waves of energy that travel from the Sun to Earth. Energy waves from the Sun have a very wide range of forms. They include X-rays (used to see inside bodies), infrared rays (used to take photos in the dark), and microwaves (used for cooking and sending cell phone signals). According to the gravitational vortex theory, crop circles are formed by microwaves.

Energy and the ionosphere

The gravitational vortex theory claims that vortexes of energy are formed in the ionosphere. But what is the ionosphere?

The ionosphere is one of several layers of gases that surround Earth. These layers are known as the upper atmosphere. The ionosphere lies between 43 miles (70 kilometers) and 250 miles (400 kilometers) above the surface of Earth.

Glossary

atmosphere mixture of gases that surround Earth

biophysics science that combines biology (the study of living things) with physics (the study of energy, sound, light, and more)

cereologist someone who investigates crop circles

charge in electricity, to pass an electric current through something that gives it an electrical energy of its own

civilization well-organized society

conclusion decision that is made after gathering and testing evidence

conduit channel through which something flows

crop formation pattern that appears in a field of crops. Crop formations can be simple circles or complex designs (pictograms).

croppie person who is very interested in crop circles. Croppies usually believe that there is a paranormal explanation for crop circles.

digit single figure

eddy small, circular current of wind

electrical current movement of electricity through wires or through the air

electromagnetic describes a wave with an energy that is created from a combination of electricity and magnetism (the power to attract some metals). There are many types of electromagnetic wave, including radio waves, X-rays, and microwaves.

evidence information and facts that help to prove something

experiment scientific test to try out a theory

Gaia force or spirit that represents all living things on planet Earth

gravitational relating to gravity, the force that pulls things down toward the surface of Earth

hoax trick

hoaxer person who tricks people on purpose

hypothesis scientific idea

ionosphere one of the layers in space, beyond Earth's atmosphere, that is a region of powerful electrical energy

microwave energy wave that creates heat

paranormal not normal and not easily explained by the laws of nature

particle very small piece

pictogram picture or design that is meant to represent an object or an idea

plasma in physics, particles that are charged with electricity

prehistoric belonging to a time before history was recorded in written form

scientific method way of testing a theory, using evidence and experiments, before reaching a conclusion

skeptic someone who doubts an idea or does not believe it

spiritual to do with beliefs and not physical things

theory idea that aims to explain something

tornado windstorm that swirls in a circle

vortex spinning flow of air or liquid

whirlwind wind that spins around very fast and moves in a tall column

Find Out More

Books

Allen, Judy. *Unexplained: An Encyclopedia of Curious Phenomena, Strange Superstitions, and Ancient Mysteries.* New York: Kingfisher, 2011.

Mason, Paul. *The Mystery of Stone Circles* (Can Science Solve?). Chicago: Heinemann Library, 2008.

Mason, Paul. *UFOs and Crop Circles* (Marvels and Mysteries). North Mankato, Minn.: Smart Apple Media, 2005.

Web sites

www.bltresearch.com/index.php
This large site includes a history of crop circles, presenting a range of different theories and reports of sightings.

www.lucypringle.co.uk/
Cereologist Lucy Pringle's web site includes her own reports, videos, and photographs.

science.howstuffworks.com/science-vs-myth/unexplained-phenomena/crop-circle3.htm
This site offers a brief introduction to crop circles.

Videos and photographs

www.temporarytemples.co.uk/milk-hill-ufo/
This is the "ball of fire" video filmed by Steve Alexander at Milk Hill, in southern England, in July 1990. It is part of a larger web site that includes many videos and photographs.

www.ukcropcircles.co.uk/
This is a photo gallery of crop circles that have appeared in the United Kingdom in the last few years.

video.nationalgeographic.com/video/places/regions-places/europe-western/uk_cropcircles/
This short video produced by National Geographic shows a range of crop circles and includes a demonstration of how crop circles can be made by using wooden boards.

Index